The Griffin Poetry Prize Anthology

The Griffin Poetry Prize Anthology

A selection of the 2001 shortlist

Edited by Esta Spalding

Published in 2001 in Canada and in the United States by
House of Anansi Press Limited
895 Don Mills Rd., 400-2 Park Centre
Toronto, ON M3C 1W3
Tel. (416) 445-3333
Fax (416) 445-5967
www.anansi.ca

Distributed in Canada by
General Distribution Services Ltd.
325 Humber College Blvd.
Etobicoke, ON M9W 7C3
Tel. (416) 213-1919
Fax (416) 213-1917
E-mail cservice@genpub.com

Distributed in the United States by
General Distribution Services Inc.
PMB 128, 4500 Witmer Industrial Estates
Niagara Falls, NY 14305-1386
Toll Free Tel. 1-800-805-1083
Toll Free Fax 1-800-481-6207
E-mail gdsinc@genpub.com

05 04 03 02 01   1 2 3 4 5

CANADIAN CATALOGUING IN PUBLICATION DATA

Main entry under title:
The Griffin poetry prize anthology

ISBN 0-88784-672-6

1. English poetry-20th century. 2. Canadian poetry (English)-20th century.
I. Spalding, Esta

PS8293.G6795 2001   821'.91408   C2001-901015-X
PR9195.25.G75 2001

Cover design: Bill Douglas @ The Bang
Typesetting: Tannice Goddard

THE CANADA COUNCIL | LE CONSEIL DES ARTS
FOR THE ARTS | DU CANADA
SINCE 1957 | DEPUIS 1957

*We acknowledge for their financial support of our publishing program the Canada
Council for the Arts, the Ontario Arts Council, and the Government of Canada
through the Book Publishing Industry Development Program (BPIDP).*

Printed and bound in Canada

Contents

The Griffin Poetry Prize Anthology

Preface

The Griffin Poetry Prize Anthology celebrates the work of the seven poets and translators shortlisted for the inaugural Griffin Poetry Prize, created by the Griffin Trust to encourage excellence in poetry written in English anywhere in the world.

The international shortlist for 2001 includes the translation by Chana Bloch and Chana Kronfeld of Yehuda Amichai's *Open Closed Open*; Fanny Howe's *Selected Poems*; Les Murray's *Learning Human: Selected Poems*; and the translation by Nikolai Popov and Heather McHugh of *Glottal Stop: 101 Poems by Paul Celan*. On the Canadian shortlist are the translation by Robert Bringhurst of Ghandl of the Qayahl Llaanas' *Nine Visits to the Mythworld*; Anne Carson's *Men in the Off Hours*; and Don McKay's *Another Gravity*. Selections from each volume are introduced here by the citation of the judges.

The Griffin Trust is a Canadian initiative, founded in April 2000 by Scott Griffin, its chair, with trustees Margaret Atwood, Robert Hass, Michael Ondaatje, Robin Robertson, and David Young. The trustees hope to help raise public awareness of the crucial role of poetry in our cultural life.

The Griffin Trust's support for poets, of poetry, and of the publishers of poetry includes two prizes worth $40,000 each. These are awarded annually for collections published in English during the preceding year. One prize goes to a living Canadian poet or translator, the other to a living poet or translator from any country, which may include Canada. This year's judges were Carolyn Forché, Dennis Lee, and Paul Muldoon. The prizes were awarded on June 7, 2001, in Toronto. This book was printed before the winners were announced, and includes, but does not identify, the Griffin Prize winners.

Royalties from *The Griffin Poetry Prize Anthology* will be donated to UNESCO's World Poetry Day, created to support linguistic diversity through poetic expression, and to offer endangered languages the opportunity to be heard in their communities.

International Finalists

Chana Bloch and Chana Kronfeld (translators)

Yehuda Amichai: *Open Closed Open*

These last poems by the greatest Israeli poet of the modern era are marked by the humanity and humour which have always characterized his work. Here they seem even more depth-charged, as when he writes, "When you go out for a night patrol, fill your canteen to the top/ so the water won't make a sloshing sound and give you away./ That's how your soul ought to be in your body, large and full and silent." The challenge of rendering the range of his tone has been met with extraordinary amplitude and aplomb by Chana Bloch and Chana Kronfeld.

The Amen Stone

On my desk there is a stone with the word "Amen" on it,
a triangular fragment of stone from a Jewish graveyard destroyed
many generations ago. The other fragments, hundreds upon hundreds,
were scattered helter-skelter, and a great yearning,
a longing without end, fills them all:
first name in search of a family name, date of death seeks
dead man's birthplace, son's name wishes to locate
name of father, date of birth seeks reunion with soul
that wishes to rest in peace. And until they have found
one another, they will not find perfect rest.
Only this stone lies calmly on my desk and says "Amen."
But now the fragments are gathered up in lovingkindness
by a sad good man. He cleanses them of every blemish,
photographs them one by one, arranges them on the floor
in the great hall, makes each gravestone whole again,
one again: fragment to fragment,
like the resurrection of the dead, a mosaic,
a jigsaw puzzle. Child's play.

I Foretell the Days of Yore

1

The flight attendants of the next millennium came to me and said:
You can still get a seat on the third millennium before liftoff.
Come with us, dead or alive, we'll take you along. We have no malice,
no defenses, but we're strong and mobile as constellations;
our eyes are closed but we can see.
We are women who glide between life and death.
You with your seat belts and gear belts and buckles that click shut,
you, sir, you with the noise of a door closing,
we with our voices of glide and whisper.
Our belts are not for safety or for holding up our clothes,
they are snakes, they are decoration. Gliding spirals,
we are acrobats looping the loops of wish and would.
You with your warm worries and emotions
heavy as cow dung in the field,
you with the sweat of your death like an afterlife perfume.

2

We are the flight attendants of the next millennium, buoyant brides
with no excess baggage of bridegrooms,
while you are weighed down by the stripes and checks on your clothing.
You with the flicking colors of traffic lights, permitted, forbidden—
for us color changes are fluid. You with your strict demarcations
of sacred and profane, outerwear and underwear; for us
everything is like water within water. You with your little excitements
and attachments, your oaths and your vows,
your buttons and snaps, your comb and your qualms,
hairbrush and despairs, you with your loneliness
and the compassion of wombs, of testicles and stiff members.
For us everything is smooth and transparent—pliable glass.
You with your conjunctions and prepositions,
you with your spirit, your respiration and resuscitation,
your distance and intimacy. We are the world to come,

come with us, we'll preserve you like a potsherd, like a symbol,
like a lion of stone, and in the year 2024
we will celebrate your hundredth birthday.

3
I am a prophet of what has already been. I read the past in the palm
of the woman I love, I forecast the winter rains that have fallen,
I am an expert on the snows of yesteryear, I conjure the spirits
of what has always been, I foretell the days of yore,
I draw up the blueprints for a house right after it's torn down,
I prophesy the small room with its few pieces of furniture—
a towel draped over the only chair to dry,
the arch of the high window, curved like our bodies in love.

4
I am a prophet of the past. And how do you see and foresee
the future? As when a man sees a woman with a beautiful body
walking before him in the street
and looks at her with desire, but she doesn't turn
to look back, just smooths her skirt a little,
pulls her blouse tight, fixes the back of her hair, then
without turning toward the man's gaze
quickens her step. That's
what the future is like.

5
Life, I think, is hard work:
As Jacob labored to be with Rachel seven years
plus seven plus seven times seven, I've worked
to be one with my life, like the beloved Rachel
and to be one with my death, like the beloved Rachel.

6
Straight from the fear of loss I plunged into the fear of being lost.
I couldn't stay long enough between them
in the sweet little no man's land of my everlasting
passing days. My hands are the hands of search and test,
hands of hope, hands of gloom,
always fumbling among papers on tables
or in drawers, in closets and in my clothes
which have seen their share of loss.
With hands that search for what is already lost, I caress your face,
and with hands afraid of loss I hold you close
and like a blind man feel my way around your eyes, your mouth,
wandering, wondering, wandering, wondering.
Because hands afraid of loss are the only hands for love.

Once I saw a violinist playing and I thought: Between
his right hand and his left—only the violin,
but what a between, what music!

7
Between the eve of the holiday and the final day
the holiday itself gets squeezed, between
longing for the past and longing for the future
the spirit is ground up as if by two heavy grindstones,
upper and lower. Between "In the East is my heart" and "I dwell
at the end of the West," the sea goes dry. Between the preventive
lament of before and the lament of after, joy shuts down.
Between hanging out flags for the holiday and folding them up again,
the wind blows and sweeps everything away.
The song of the turtledove mourning is the song
of the turtledove wooing. With the same body
that stoops to pick up a fallen something from the floor,
I bow down to God. That is my faith, my religion.

8

8
Counting, counting, I hear them counting
as if out for the count at the end of the fight. When I was born
they counted to ten and they went on counting.
Now the referees and the crowd have gone home,
the lights in the arena are off, I got up long ago and headed
for my life, and they are still counting.
The pleasant evening breeze is only the towel
the trainer waves in my face, believing
I'll keep up the fight. Counting, counting I hear,
sometimes out loud, sometimes in a whisper
or in a woman's voice making love, sometimes counting
like taking inventory, taking a blood count or a pulse.
Sometimes a countdown or a count-up into the future,
in a solo voice or in unison, like a Greek chorus.
And they go on counting, deciphering ciphers before
my death and after it, counting
the spheres of the stars and the uppermost spheres,
those heights so high
the singing can have no end.

9
At times I think life is like a terrible accident,
a car rolling off the road down into the abyss, slow or fast.
I roll and reconcile,
reconcile and roll.

10
Life, I think, is a series of rehearsals
for the real show. In a rehearsal you can still
make changes, cut out a sentence, add a line of dialogue, switch
actors, directors, theaters—up until the real show.
Then there is no changing. And it makes no difference

that you can't make a difference:
The show closes right after opening night.

11

All the motions and the positions in my body—
it's already been done.
I sit on a chair and think like Rodin's Thinker.
Ever since I sat folded up in my mother's belly,
I have carried inside me the wisdom of the folding chair.
My arms are raised like Moses' arms when he raised the Tablets of
    the Law,
my arms are raised without holding a thing,
a bit in disbelief, a bit in despair.
I give hugs like King David on the roof, or helpless hugs
like Jesus on the cross, but the palms of my hands
are free, I am free, though everything
has already come to pass. I have learned to swim
in the stream of consciousness, and I know a thing or two
about the difference between wire and wireless, God and
No-God, jet and chopper, a door
that opens and closes with a slam
and a revolving door that keeps revolving.

12

Now after many years of living I begin to see
that I rebelled only a little, and I do observe
all the laws and commandments.
I observe the law of gravity, that is, the law of the earth's attraction,
with all my body and with all my might and with all my love;
I observe the law of equilibrium and the law of the conservation
    of matter:
my body and my body, my soul and my soul, my body and my soul.
I abhor a vacuum in my pain and in my joy

I follow the law of water seeking its own level; past and future
are recycled back to me. I rise and I raise with the law of the lever.
I begin to understand, as I would with an old car,
what makes it work, the action of pistons and brakes,
reward and punishment, be fruitful and multiply,
forget and remember, bolts and springs,
fast and slow, and the laws of history.
Thus spake the years of my life unto the days of my life,
thus spake my soul unto the parts of my body.
This is a sermon in the synagogue, this is a eulogy
for the dead, this is burial and this
is resurrection. Thus spake the man.

Houses (Plural); Love (Singular)

1

Sheltered by good news,
sheltered even by the bad, now we are at home.
But we remain as we were then, before we had a home,
when we were in the wadis of Ein Gedi. We are still
like those wadis, you the Rejeh, I the Sideir, even now,
sheltered in our home in Jerusalem. At our door
the two eunuchs, Time and Fate, stand guard,
and the mezuzah on our doorpost says:
And thou, man, shalt love;
and thou, woman, shalt love.

2

We lived in many houses and left remnants of memory
in every one of them: a newspaper, a book face-down, a crumpled map
of some faraway land, a forgotten toothbrush standing sentinel in a cup—
that too is a memorial candle, an eternal light.

3

And in those days before we made a home for ourselves,
we made the whole country into homes.
Even the beach at Caesarea
where we piled our clothes onto a solemn mound,
sandals and shirts and towels and pants, yours and mine,
jumbled together, like us, and then went into the water.
I said to myself: If we'd lived in ancient times and made love
in the mountains or the desert, we'd have piled stone on stone
and called upon the name of the Lord and gone on our way,
but we made love by the sea, our clothes
a mound of witness in the sand,
and we called upon the name of our love.
Passersby thought we might have drowned in the sea.

But we did not drown in the sea, we drowned in all the years
after that chapter, still wrapped up
in each other, like our clothes on that mound on the shore.

4
We lived in the Valley of Gehenna in no man's land in the divided
    Jerusalem.
Our roof was hit, our walls wounded by bullets and shrapnel.
We propped up the broken leg of the bed with a pile of books.
(I don't know if we ever read them again.) The stone steps
were like the ladder the angels left behind when they fled
Jacob's dream, a ladder for us to climb up and down.
In Hebrew, no man's land is called "the zone of abandon."
When we lived there, we were a man and a woman earnest in our loving,
we were not abandoned. And if we have not died, we are loving still.

5
And if we have died, we will be first in line at the resurrection
that Ezekiel prophesied in his vision:
bones coming together, bone to bone, skin over flesh and sinew—
Ezekiel didn't go into detail. But the two of us continued his vision:
hips for hugging, soft inner thighs for stroking, twin buttocks, upper
and nether hair, eyes to open and close, lips chiseled, the tongue precise.
And we fleshed out his vision even further:
two people talking, a summer dress, underwear hung out to dry,
    a windowsill.
We will be ourselves, we will ebb and flow, changing weathers,
seasons of the year, we will go on being,
we will go on and on.

Fanny Howe

Selected Poems

Fanny Howe's lyric meditations on matter and spirit, the soul exiled, and the wondrous strangeness of human life on earth are akin to Dickinson's in their fierce wit, musicality and intelligence. Gathered from nine of her books spanning more than two decades, these poems articulate the inquisitive grace and courage of a secular contemplative, restoring to language its power to question the sacred in the interests of corporeal joy.

■

I'd speak if I wasn't afraid of inhaling
A memory I want to forget
Like I trusted the world which wasn't mine
The hollyhock in the tall vase is wide awake
And feelings are only overcome by fleeing
To their opposite. Moisture and dirt
Have entered the space between threshold and floor
A lot is my estimate when I step on it
Sorrow can be a home to stand on so
And see far to: another earth, a place I might know

■

I may never see the Vatican or Troy
but only let me sit in a car somewhere
I recognize as home by the hand
of the one I love in mine—

just once—O universe—one more time

■

The wildness of the flower is all in the tone
Where the yellow goldenrod's a chirrup

When its chaperone is sleeping, Queen Anne's Lace
appears beside chicory, seemingly for beauty's sake

And one wild rose, the last,
before October, blackens on the bush, the bees

have headed off to the thistle factory
It's audible, if you see it—

color & strain of voice, among purples,
an indifferent shoulder (rocks) raised to dim

the passionate voice

■

Three bags of gold, a fairytale—
says "there's three of everything
in this world," but don't ask why.
Three bags ablaze, but manageable

One is browner, rich and red
This is the bag of dream-analysis

One is pale yellow, or off-white, and this
represents the wish

The third is a glittering heap
of nuggets like some autumn tree

glimpsed in a sun's late mist
vulgar & true, this is the big

bag, the bag of forgetfulness
which lasts

till the weight of it breaks

■

God is already ahead and waiting: the future is full.
One steps timidly over the world;
the other is companionable.
The house is there. The door is there . . . others . . .
But for you they make no sound when you're so far.
I know the bench is by the pond tomorrow
when I can follow the streets to it by heart.
Yes, streets. Yes, heart.
Nightwalk of faith, chromosomes live in the past.
The land is an incarnation
like a hand on a hand on an arm asking *do you know me?*

■

Zero built a nest
In my navel. Incurable
Longing. Blood too—

From violent actions
It's a nest belonging to one
But zero uses it
And its pleasure is its own

■

Go on out but come back in
you told me to live by, so I went
with my little dog trotting

at my side out of the garden
into woods colored rotten.

I did this several times, out and in,
it was of course a meditation.

The out surrounds me now
a whole invisible O to live in:

tender tantrums, sky gone suddenly gray—
still soften light but no one brings

papers here to sign. The top of the water
shudders under the brush of wind.

Past? Present? Future? No such things.

■

Rain—red rhododendron tree—
whitethorn—drumlin—you and me—
a hum of bees—tea—
white milk—brown sugar—bread—honey—
waterdrops—later afternoon sun—near Drum.

Inside me, a pulse of desire.
Inside me, the way elsewhere.

■

Into the forest I went walking—to get lost.

I saw faces in the knots
of trees, it was insane, and hands
in branches, and everywhere names.

Throughout the elms
small birds shivered and sang
in rhyme.

I wanted to be air, or wind—to be at ease
in outer space but in the world
this was the case:

Human was God's secret name.

■

I won't be able to write from the grave
so let me tell you what I love:
oil, vinegar, salt, lettuce, brown bread, butter,
cheese and wine, a windy day, a fireplace,
the children nearby, poems and songs,
a friend sleeping in my bed—

and the short northern nights.

Les Murray

Learning Human: Selected Poems

This is a generous selection of poems, written over a period of thirty-five years by the preeminent Australian poet of the late twentieth century. Les Murray has a sure touch with the long leisurely poem, written in panavision and what he celebrates in "The Quality of Sprawl" — "Sprawl is doing your farming by aeroplane, roughly,/ or driving a hitchhiker that extra hundred miles home." Murray is also good on the Polaroid snapshot — of an oyster, for instance, with its "bloodless sheep's eye." Whether he's running a marathon or the hundred meters, Murray gives us beauty and bounty in equal measures.

An Absolutely Ordinary Rainbow

The word goes round Repins,
the murmur goes round Lorenzinis,
at Tattersalls, men look up from sheets of numbers,
the Stock Exchange scribblers forget the chalk in their hands
and men with bread in their pockets leave the Greek Club:
There's a fellow crying in Martin Place. They can't stop him.

The traffic in George Street is banked up for half a mile
and drained of motion. The crowds are edgy with talk
and more crowds come hurrying. Many run in the back streets
which minutes ago were busy main streets, pointing:
There's a fellow weeping down there. No one can stop him.

The man we surround, the man no one approaches
simply weeps, and does not cover it, weeps
not like a child, not like the wind, like a man
and does not declaim it, nor beat his breast, nor even
sob very loudly—yet the dignity of his weeping

holds us back from his space, the hollow he makes about him
in the midday light, in his pentagram of sorrow,
and uniforms back in the crowd who tried to seize him
stare out at him, and feel, with amazement, their minds
longing for tears as children for a rainbow.

Some will say, in the years to come, a halo
or force stood around him. There is no such thing.
Some will say they were shocked and would have stopped him
but they will not have been there. The fiercest manhood,
the toughest reserve, the slickest wit amongst us

trembles with silence, and burns with unexpected
judgements of peace. Some in the concourse scream
who thought themselves happy. Only the smallest children
and such as look out of Paradise come near him
and sit at his feet, with dogs and dusty pigeons.

Ridiculous, says a man near me, and stops
his mouth with his hands, as if it uttered vomit—
and I see a woman, shining, stretch her hand
and shake as she receives the gift of weeping:
as many as follow her also receive it

and many weep for sheer acceptance, and more
refuse to weep for fear of all acceptance,
but the weeping man, like the earth, requires nothing,
the man who weeps ignores us, and cries out
of his writhen face and ordinary body

not words, but grief, not messages, but sorrow,
hard as the earth, sheer, present as the sea—
and when he stops, he simply walks between us
mopping his face with the dignity of one
man who has wept, and now has finished weeping.

Evading believers, he hurries off down Pitt Street.

The Quality of Sprawl

Sprawl is the quality
of the man who cut down his Rolls-Royce
into a farm utility truck, and sprawl
is what the company lacked when it made repeated efforts
to buy the vehicle back and repair its image.

Sprawl is doing your farming by aeroplane, roughly,
or driving a hitchhiker that extra hundred miles home.
It is the rococo of being your own still centre.
It is never lighting cigars with ten-dollar notes:
that's idiot ostentation and murder of starving people.
Nor can it be bought with the ash of million-dollar deeds.

Sprawl lengthens the legs; it trains greyhounds on liver and beer.
Sprawl almost never says Why not? with palms comically raised
nor can it be dressed for, not even in running shoes worn
with mink and a nose ring. That is Society. That's Style.
Sprawl is more like the thirteenth banana in a dozen
or anyway the fourteenth.

Sprawl is Hank Stamper in *Never Give an Inch*
bisecting an obstructive official's desk with a chainsaw.
Not harming the official. Sprawl is never brutal
though it's often intransigent. Sprawl is never Simon de Montfort
at a town-storming: Kill them all! God will know his own.
Knowing the man's name this was said to might be sprawl.

Sprawl occurs in art. The fifteenth to twenty-first
lines in a sonnet, for example. And in certain paintings;
I have sprawl enough to have forgotten which paintings.
Turner's glorious *Burning of the Houses of Parliament*
comes to mind, a doubling bannered triumph of sprawl—
except, he didn't fire them.

Sprawl gets up the nose of many kinds of people
(every kind that comes in kinds) whose futures don't include it.
Some decry it as criminal presumption, silken-robed Pope
    Alexander
dividing the new world between Spain and Portugal.
If he smiled *in petto* afterwards, perhaps the thing did have sprawl.

Sprawl is really classless, though. It's John Christopher Frederick
    Murray
asleep in his neighbours' best bed in spurs and oilskins
but not having thrown up:
sprawl is never Calum who, drunk, along the hallways of our
    house,
reinvented the Festoon. Rather
it's Beatrice Miles going twelve hundred ditto in a taxi,
No Lewd Advances, No Hitting Animals, No Speeding,
on the proceeds of her two-bob-a-sonnet Shakespeare readings.
An image of my country. And would that it were more so.

No, sprawl is full-gloss murals on a council-house wall.
Sprawl leans on things. It is loose-limbed in its mind.
Reprimanded and dismissed
it listens with a grin and one boot up on the rail
of possibility. It may have to leave the Earth.
Being roughly Christian, it scratches the other cheek
and thinks it unlikely. Though people have been shot for sprawl.

Nocturne

Brisbane, night-gathered, far away
estuarine imaginary city
of houses towering down one side
of slatted lights seen under leaves

confluence of ranginess with lush,
Brisbane, of rotogravure memory
approached by web lines of coke and grit
by sleepers racked in corridor trains

weatherboard incantatory city
of the timber duchess, the strapped port
in Auchenflower and Fortitude Valley
and bottletops spat in Vulture Street

greatest of the floodtime towns
that choked the dictionary with silt
and hung a navy in the tropic gardens.
Brisbane, on the steep green slope to war

brothel-humid headquarters city
where commandos and their allies fought
down café stairs, belt buckle and boot
and once with a rattletrap green gun.

In midnight nets, in mango bombings
Brisbane, storied and cable-fixed,
above your rum river, farewell and adieu
in marble on the hill of Toowong

by golfing pockets, by deep squared pockets
night heals the bubbled tar of day
and the crab moon, rising, reddens above
Brisbane, rotating far away.

The Tin Wash Dish

Lank poverty, dank poverty,
its pants wear through at fork and knee.
It warms its hands over burning shames,
refers to its fate as Them and He
and delights in things by their hard names:
rag and toejam, feed and paw—
don't guts that down, there ain't no more!
Dank poverty, rank poverty,
it hums with a grim fidelity
like wood-rot with a hint of orifice,
wet newspaper jammed in the gaps of artifice,
and disgusts us into fierce loyalty.
It's never the fault of those you love:
poverty comes down from above.
Let it dance chairs and smash the door,
it arises from all that went before
and every outsider's the enemy—
Jesus Christ turned this over with his stick
and knights and philosophers turned it back.
Rank poverty, lank poverty,
chafe in its crotch and sores in its hair,
still a window's clean if it's made of air
and not webbed silver like a sleeve.
Watch out if this does well at school
and has to leave and longs to leave:
someone, sometime, will have to pay.
Lank poverty, dank poverty,
the cornbag quilt breeds such loyalty.
Shave with toilet soap, run to flesh,
astound the nation, run the army,
still you wait for the day you'll be sent back
where books or toys on the floor are rubbish
and no one's allowed to come and play
because home calls itself a shack
and hot water crinkles in the tin wash dish.

The Cows on Killing Day

All me are standing on feed. The sky is shining.

All me have just been milked. Teats all tingling still
from that dry toothless sucking by the chilly mouths
that gasp loudly in in in, and never breathe out.

All me standing on feed, move the feed inside me.
One me smells of needing the bull, that heavy urgent me,
the back-climber, who leaves me humped, straining, but light
and peaceful again, with crystalline moving inside me.

Standing on wet rock, being milked, assuages the calf-sorrow in me.
Now the me who needs mounts on me, hopping, to signal the bull.

The tractor comes trotting in its grumble; the heifer human
bounces on top of it, and cud comes with the tractor,
big rolls of tight dry feed: lucerne, clovers, buttercup, grass,
that's been bitten but never swallowed, yet is cud.
She walks up over the tractor and down it comes, roll on roll
and all me following, eating it, and dropping the good pats.

The heifer human smells of needing the bull human
and is angry. All me look nervously at her
as she chases the dog me dream of horning dead: our enemy
of the light loose tongue. Me'd jam him in his squeals.

Me, facing every way, spreading out over feed.

One me is still in the yard, the place skinned of feed.
Me, old and sore-boned, little milk in that me now,
licks at the wood. The oldest bull human is coming.

Me in the peed yard. A stick goes out from the human
and cracks, like the whip. Me shivers and falls down

with the terrible, the blood of me, coming out behind an ear.
Me, that other me, down and dreaming in the bare yard.

All me come running. It's like the Hot Part of the sky
that's hard to look at, this that now happens behind wood
in the raw yard. A shining leaf, like off the bitter gum tree
is with the human. It works in the neck of me
and the terrible floods out, swamped and frothy. All me make the Roar,
some leaping stiff-kneed, trying to horn that worst horror.
The wolf-at-the-calves is the bull human. Horn the bull human!

But the dog and the heifer human drive away all me.

Looking back, the glistening leaf is still moving.
All of dry old me is crumpled, like the hills of feed,
and a slick me like a huge calf is coming out of me.

The carrion-stinking dog, who is calf of human and wolf,
is chasing and eating little blood things the humans scatter,
and all me run away, over smells, toward the sky.

The International Terminal

Some comb oil, some blow air,
some shave trenchlines in their hair
but the common joint thump, the heart's spondee
kicks off in its rose-lit inner sea
like an echo, at first, of the one above
it on the dodgy ladder of love—
and my mate who's driving says, *I never
found one yet worth staying with forever.*
In this our poems do not align.
Surely most are if you are, answers mine,
and I am living proof of it,
I gloom, missing you from the cornering outset—
and hearts beat mostly as if they weren't there,
rocking horse to rocking chair,
most audible dubbed on the tracks of movies
or as we approach where our special groove is
or our special fear. The autumn-vast
parking-lot-bitumen overcast
now switches on pumpkin-flower lights
all over dark green garden sites
and a wall of car-bodies, stacked by blokes,
obscures suburban signs and smokes.
Like coughs, cries, all such unlearned effects
the heartbeat has no dialects
but what this or anything may mean
depends on what poem we're living in.
Now a jet engine, huge child of a gun,
shudders with haze and begins to run.
Over Mount Fuji and the North Pole
I'm bound for Europe in a reading role
and a poem long ago that was coming for me
had Fuji-san as its axle-tree.
Cities shower and rattle over the gates
as I enter that limbo between states
but I think of the heart swarmed round by poems

like an egg besieged by chromosomes
and how out of that our world is bred
through the back of a mirror, with clouds in its head
—and airborne, with a bang, this five-hundred-seat
theatre folds up its ponderous feet.

Nikolai Popov and Heather McHugh (translators)

Glottal Stop: 101 Poems by Paul Celan

Paul Celan is arguably the most important European poet of the twentieth century, but much of his work has seemed too hermetic, linguistically complex, and bound to his struggle with the German language in the aftermath of the Shoah to be translatable. In *Glottal Stop*, however, Nikolai Popov and Heather McHugh have achieved the seemingly impossible: more than translating Celan into English, they have found a way to translate English into Celan.

■

Voices, scored into
the waters' green.
When the kingfisher dives,
the split second whirs:

What stood by you
appears on every shore
mown down
into another image.

* * *

Voices from the nettles:

Come to us on your hands.
All you can read, alone
with a lamp, is your palm.

* * *

Voices, night-knotted, ropes
on which you hang your bell.

Dome yourself over, world:
when death's shell washes up on shore
a bell will want to ring.

* * *

Voices that make your heart
recoil into your mother's.
Voices from the hanging-tree
where old growth and young growth
exchange rings.

* * *

Voices, guttural, amid the debris,
where even infinity shovels,
runnels of
(cardio-) slime.

Launch here the boats I manned,
my son.

Amidships, when an evil wind takes charge,
the clamps and brackets close.

Jacob's voice:

The tears.
Tears in the eye of my brother.
One clung. It grew.
We live in there.
Now, breathe—
so it may
fall.

* * *

Voices inside the ark:

Only
the mouths
were saved. Hear us,
o sinking things.

* * *

No
voice—
late noise, stranger to the hour,
gift to your thoughts, born of
wakefulness here in the final
account: a
carpel, large as an eye, and deeply
scored: bleeds
sap, and won't
heal over.

■

With wine and being lost, with
less and less of both:

I rode through the snow, do you read me,
I rode God far—I rode God
near, he sang,
it was
our last ride over
the hurdled humans.

They cowered when
they heard us
overhead, they
wrote, they
lied our neighing
into one of their
image-ridden languages.

■

Flung wood
on the windpipe's path,
so it goes, wing-
powered,
true,
taking off
along star-trails, kissed
by world-
shards, scarred
by time-
grains, time-dust,
your orphan sibling, lapilli, turned
dwarf, turned tiny, turned
to nothing,
gone away and done away, self-
rhyme—
and so it comes
back home,
in its turn re-
turns, to
hover on
a heartbeat, one
millennium, the only
hand on the dial
that one
soul—its own soul—
described, that
one
soul numbers
now.

■

Crackpots, decomposing
deeps.

If I were—

well, yes, if
I were that ash tree—bent
which way?—outside

I'd be able to
go along with you,
bright pan of gray, you and
the image growing through you
only at once to be
choked down,
and the two of you
caught
in the flashy, tight-drawn
noose of thought.

■

The sight of the songbirds at dusk,
through a ring of
ungraphed space,

made me promise myself weapons.

The sight of weapons, hands;
the sight of hands, the line
long since described by a flat, sharp
rock,

—you, wave,
carried it here, sharpened it,
you, Un-
losable One, gave yourself to it,
you, beach-sand, are the taker,
partaker,
you, shore-grass, drift
your share—

the line, the line
we swim through, twice each
millennium, tied up
in each other,
and not even the sea,
sublime unfathomable sea
that runs alive through us,
can believe
all the singing in our fingers.

■

Coincidence staged, the signs all
unconsigned to wind, the number
multiplied, wrongs wreathed,
the Lord a closet-fugitive, rainfaller, eyeballer,
as lies turn blazing sevens, knives
turn flatterers, crutches
perjurors, U-
under
        this
                world,
the ninth one is already tunneling,
    O Lion,
sing the human song of
tooth and soul, the two
hard things.

■

Here are the industrious
mineral resources (domestic)

here the heated-up syncope

here the insoluble riddle
of the jubilee year

here the glassed-in
spider altars in the facility's
overarching sprawl

here the half-sounds
(still there?),
shades' palaver

here the ice-adjusted fears
cleared for flight

here the semantically X-rayed
sound-proof shower-room,
with its baroque appointments

here the unscrawled wall
of a cell:

live your life right
through here, without a clock.

■

O little root of a dream
you hold me here
undermined by blood,
no longer visible to anyone,
property of death.

Curve a face
that there may be speech, of earth,
of ardor, of
things with eyes, even
here, where you read me blind,

even
here,
where you
refute me,
to the letter.

Canadian Finalists

Robert Bringhurst
(translator)

Ghandl of the Qayahl Llaanas: *Nine Visits
to the Mythworld*

For most readers, *Nine Visits to the Mythworld* will be
a revelation. These sophisticated narrative poems by the
Haida mythteller Ghandl come from an unfamiliar
imaginative world, studied by specialists more for its
anthropological interest than its artistry. Robert
Bringhurst's sinewy language and acute formal
intelligence now reveal poetry of vivacity and stature,
which can be enjoyed as a cultural treasure.

The Way the Weather Chose to Be Born

There was a child of good family, they say,   I
at Swiftcurrent Creek.
And her father had one of his slaves
        constantly watching her.
She said to the slave,
«Tell that one I want to make love to him.»

The day after that,
        when she went out of doors with the slave,
she asked if he'd said
what she told him to say.

And the slave said to the young woman,
«He says he's afraid of your father.»
But the slave had spoken to no one.
The slave was in love with her, they say.

When she had decided on somebody else,
she gave the slave the same instructions.
He failed again to deliver the message.
He told her again
that the man was afraid of her father.

After sending the message to each of her father's ten nephews,
the one of good family made love with the slave, they say.
And her father found out it had happened.

So they all moved away from her, they say.
And no one but her youngest uncle's wife
        left food for her, they say.

She went digging for shellfish, they say.   2.1
After a while, she dug up a cockleshell.
The cry of a child came from inside it.

She looked at it closely.
The embryo of a child was living inside it.
She carried it into the house.
She put birds' down around it.

Then, though she gave it no milk,
it grew very quickly.
Soon it started crawling
Soon after that it was walking.

One day the child said,   2.2
«Mother, like this.»
He was gesturing with his hands.
When he did it again,
she knew what he wanted.

She hammered a copper bracelet into a bow.
She hammered another one into an arrow.
After she finished a second arrow,
she gave him the weapons.
Then he was happy.

And then he went hunting for birds.
He came back with a cormorant for his mother.
She ate it.

The next day again he went hunting for birds,
and he brought in a goose for his mother, they say.
She ate it.

The next day again he went hunting for birds.
He brought in a wren.
He skinned it himself,
and he dried the skin.
He cherished it.

Next day, he brought in a song sparrow.
This too he skinned by himself,
and he dried the skin.

The next day he brought in a Steller's jay,
and he skinned it
and dried it.

The day after that, he brought in a redheaded sapsucker.
He skinned it as well,
and he dried it.

Then in the night something spoke to his mother.   2.3
Just at that moment, the house started creaking.
Next morning he woke in a well-finished building.
The carvings on the houseposts winked their eyes.
Master Carver had adopted him, they say.

He got up.
And his father said to him,
«Well, my young lord, let me paint you.»

He went to his father.
His father put level streaks of cloud on his face.
«Now, my young lord, sit facing the sea.»
And the moment he did so, the weather was fine.

Then one day he asked his father
to come with him on a fishing trip, they say.
«We're going to catch the fish-catching octopus.»
And he fished for it and he caught it.

3

They drifted with the current over House Banks.
He told his father to sit in the bow.
He looked at the rising sun for a while.

Then he said, «Father, say this:
The Largest One of Them All is thinking of biting.»
His father said these very words.

«Father, say this:
*The One Who Travels All around the Islands
    is thinking of biting.*»
And he spoke these very words.

«Father, say *Sir, shadows are falling on Steep Rock Mountain.
Make up your mind.*»
And he spoke these very words.

«Father, say this:
*The Big One Who Comes to Swiftcurrent Creek
    is thinking of biting.*»
And he said those very words.

«Father, say this:
The Big One Slurping Up Pebbles is thinking of biting.»
He said it.

And then, «Father, say this:
The One with White Stone Eyes has looked it over.»

«Father, say this:
The Big One Who Feeds Wherever He Pleases
 is thinking of biting.»
He said these very words.

As soon as he had said these things,
it took the bait, they say.
And then it towed them right around the Islands.

He slapped the canoe on the gunwales, they say.
And he said to it,
«Master Carver made you.
Swim with your head up.»
Then it towed them round the Islands once again.

When they came to rest,
he hauled in the line.
And he brought to the surface the face
     of something amazing.

A forest of broad-bladed kelp surrounded its mouth.
There were halibut nesting all over it.
Then, they say, he started to bring them aboard.

He filled his canoe.
Then he stretched it out larger.
He kept on hauling them aboard,
and he again filled his canoe.
Then they released it.

They paddled back to town in their canoe.
Master Carver brought the halibut up to his wife.
She cut it and dried it.

Then he called his son once more, they say.
And after he had painted him, he said,
«My son, your uncles are living in that direction.
Go there and see.»
And he went there, they say.

At the edge of the town, he sat down.
When he had sat there awhile, they saw him.
They crowded around him.

They knew him at once, they say.
And then they moved back where his mother was living.

W hen all of them had lived there for a while,   4.1
he went out of the house
            dressed in his wren skin, they say.
«Come look at me, mother,» he said.
And his mother followed him outside.
She saw him poised above the sea as a cumulus cloud.

Then they came in,
and he said to his mother,
«Did I look handsome?»
«Yes, my young lord, you looked fine.»

Next, they say, he went out in the skin of the Steller's jay.
And he said to his mother,
«Come look at me.»
She followed him outside.
Above the sea, her son was spread out wide and blue.

Then they came in,
and he said, «Did I look handsome, mother?»
«Yes, my young lord, you looked fine.»

Then he went out in his sapsucker skin.
And he said, «Come look at me, mother.»
His mother followed him outside.
He was bright red high above the sea.

She smiled at her son.
When they came back in, he said,
«Did I look handsome, mother?»
«Yes, my young lord.
The gods will never grow tired of seeing your face.»

«This is the last I will see of you, mother,» he said.
«I am going away.
Whenever I sit where the Tallgrass River reaches the sea,
no wind will blow from any direction.
The sky will be mine.

«Whenever my face is the same as my father painted it,
no wind will blow from any direction.
Humans will feed themselves through me.»

«Very well, my young lord.
Whenever you sit there,
I will scatter feathers in your honor.»

Then he left his mother, they say.   4.2
And his father got ready to leave her as well.

«I also am going away,» he said.
«Make your home at the headwaters.
I will be watching for you there,
and I will also be watching for my son.»
Then he left her there, they say.

As the day was ending,   4.3
she called her youngest uncle aside.
«Tomorrow,» she said,
      «when you and your brothers go fishing,
wear a new hat
and take a new paddle.»

And early next day, they all went out fishing.
She sat at the end of the town
and stretched out her legs.
When she pulled up her skirt,
the wind blew out of the inlet.

The higher she raised it, the fiercer the wind.
When her skirt came up over her knees,
a gale was blowing.

And she clung to the thread
of the one who wore a new hat.
She saved him, they say, and him only,
because of his wife, who had left her some food.
She is Fairweather Woman, they say.

Then she went inland, they say,   5
taking her mats and all her belongings.
She walked up the bed of the creek,
and she settled there.

Later a trail was cut over top of her.
The traffic disturbed her, she said,
and she moved farther inland.
She sank to her buttocks, they say.
There, they say, she is one with the ground.

When her son takes his place,
she scatters flakes of snow for him.
Those are the feathers.

That is the end.

Anne Carson

Men in the Off Hours

Anne Carson continues to redefine what a book of poetry can be; this ambitious collection ranges from quatrains studded with uncanny images ("Here lies the refugee breather/ who drank a bowl of elsewhere") to musing verse essays, personal laments, rigorous classical scholarship, and meditations on artists' lives, caught in the carnage of history. All are burnished by Carson's dialectical imagination, and her quizzical, stricken moral sense.

Epitaph: Zion

Murderous little world once our objects had gazes. Our lives
      Were fragile, the wind
Could dash them away. Here lies the refugee breather
      Who drank a bowl of elsewhere.

New Rule

A New Year's white morning of hard new ice.
High on the frozen branches I saw a squirrel jump and skid.
Is this scary? he seemed to say and glanced

down at me, clutching his branch as it bobbed
in stiff recoil—or is it just that everything sounds wrong today?
The branches

clinked.
He wiped his small cold lips with one hand.
Do you fear the same things as

I fear? I countered, looking up.
His empire of branches slid against the air.
The night of hooks?

The man blade left open on the stair?
Not enough spin on it, said my true love
when he left in our fifth year.

The squirrel bounced down a branch
and caught a peg of tears.
The way to hold on is

afterwords
so
clear.

Father's Old Blue Cardigan

Now it hangs on the back of the kitchen chair
where I always sit, as it did
on the back of the kitchen chair where he always sat.

I put it on whenever I come in,
as he did, stamping
the snow from his boots.

I put it on and sit in the dark.
He would not have done this.
Coldness comes paring down from the moonbone in the sky.

His laws were a secret.
But I remember the moment at which I knew
he was going mad inside his laws.

He was standing at the turn of the driveway when I arrived.
He had on the blue cardigan with the buttons done up all the way to the top.
Not only because it was a hot July afternoon

but the look on his face—
as a small child who has been dressed by some aunt early in the morning
for a long trip

on cold trains and windy platforms
will sit very straight at the edge of his seat
while the shadows like long fingers

over the haystacks that sweep past
keep shocking him
because he is riding backwards.

TV Men: Sappho

avec ma main brûlée j'écris sur la nature du feu

I.

No one knows what the laws are. That there are laws
we know, by the daily burnings if nothing else.
On the second

day of shooting in the Place de la Concorde
I notice the leaves in the Jardin have changed
overnight,

but mention this to no one
for fear of continuity problems.
I had already invalidated 16 (otherwise good)

takes this morning by changing an earring.
You cannot erase.
Is this a law?

No, a talent. To step obliquely
where stones are sharp.
Vice is also sharp.

There are laws against vice.
But the shock stays with you.

II.

la vie est brève
un peu d'amour
un peu de rêve
ainsi bonjour

The Talent has a talent
for the obvious.
See this rope?

Tie one end to me
and the other to Death:
overlit on all fours I shall

circle Him
at a consistent focal length.
Not too close not too far—

("Home," whispers the cameraman)
as the gravestones in the background
spill slowly

out of the frame.
Earth will be warmer than we thought,
after all this circling.

TV Men: Lazarus

Yes I admit a degree of unease about my
motives in making
this documentary.
Mere prurience of a kind that is all too common nowadays
in public catastrophes. I was listening

to a peace negotiator for the Balkans talk
about his vocation
on the radio the other day.
"We drove down through this wasteland and I didn't know
much about the area but I was

fascinated by the horrors of it. I had never
seen a thing like this.
I videotaped it.
Then sent a 13-page memo to the UN with my suggestions."
This person was a member

of the International Rescue Committee,
not a man of TV.
But you can see
how the pull is irresistible. The pull to handle horrors
and to have a theory of them.

But now I see my assistant producer waving her arms
at me to get
on with the script.
The name Lazarus is an abbreviated form of Hebrew 'El'azar,
meaning "God has helped."

I have long been interested in those whom God has helped.
It seems often to be the case,
e.g. with saints or martyrs,
that God helps them to far more suffering than they would have
without God's help. But then you get

someone like Lazarus, a man of no
particular importance,
on whom God bestows
the ultimate benevolence, without explanation, then abandons
him again to his nonentity.

We are left wondering, *Why Lazarus?*
My theory is
God wants us to wonder this.
After all, if there were some quality that Lazarus possessed,
some criterion of excellence

by which he was chosen to be called
back
from death,
then we would all start competing to achieve this.
But if

God's gift is simply random, well
for one thing
it makes a
more interesting TV show. God's choice can be seen emerging
from the dark side of reason

like a new planet. No use being historical
about this planet,
it is just an imitation.
As Lazarus is an imitation of Christ. As TV is an imitation of
Lazarus. As you and I are an imitation of

TV. Already you notice that
although I am merely
a director of photography,
I have grasped certain fundamental notions first advanced by Plato,
e.g. that our reality is just a TV set

inside a TV set inside a TV set, with nobody watching
but Sokrates,
who changed
the channel in 399 B.C. But my bond with Lazarus goes deeper, indeed
nausea overtakes me when faced with

the prospect of something simply beginning all over again.
Each time I have to
raise my slate and say
"Take 12!" or "Take 13!" and then "Take 14!"
I cannot restrain a shudder.

Repetition is horrible. Poor Lazarus cannot have known
he was an
imitation Christ,
but who can doubt he realized, soon after being ripped out of his
warm little bed in the ground,

his own epoch of repetition just beginning.
Lazarus Take 2!
Poor drop.
As a bit of salt falls back down the funnel. Or maybe my pity
is misplaced. Some people think Lazarus lucky,

like Samuel Beckett who calls him "Happy Larry" or Rilke
who speaks of
that moment in a game
when "the pure too-little flips over into the empty too-much."
Well I am now explaining why my documentary

focuses entirely on this moment, the flip-over moment.
Before and after
don't interest me.
You won't be seeing any clips from home videos of Lazarus
in short pants racing his sisters up a hill.

No footage of Mary and Martha side by side on the sofa
discussing how they manage
at home
with a dead one sitting down to dinner. No panel of experts
debating who was really the victim here.

Our sequence begins and ends with that moment of complete
innocence
and sport—
when Lazarus licks the first drop of afterlife off the nipple
of his own old death.

I put tiny microphones all over the ground
to pick up
the magic
of the vermin in his ten fingers and I stand back to wait
for the miracle.

Epitaph: Thaw

Little clicks all night in the back lane there blackness
      Goes leaking out the key.
"It twindles," said Father to April on her
      Anvil of deep decree.

Don McKay

Another Gravity

Don McKay's journey through closely observed places and creatures not only brings them alive with great panache, it explores a more humane way of living on earth, "bereft and happy, my whole mind/ applauding." These wonderfully bittersweet poems establish a rich vocabulary of dwelling — of "lift and drag," of homing and leaving home. The result is a playful yet resonant microcosm, charted with virtuosity and love.

Sometimes a Voice (1)

Sometimes a voice – have you heard this? –
wants not to be voice any longer, wants something
whispering between the words, some
rumour of its former life. Sometimes, even
in the midst of making sense or conversation, it will
hearken back to breath, or even farther,
to the wind, and recognize itself
as troubled air, a flight path still
looking for its bird.
                          I'm thinking of us up there
shingling the boathouse roof. That job is all
off balance – squat, hammer, body skewed
against the incline, heft the bundle,
daub the tar, squat. Talking,
as we always talked, about not living
past the age of thirty with its
labyrinthine perils: getting hooked,
steady job, kids, business suit. Fuck that. The roof
sloped upward like a take-off ramp
waiting for Evel Knievel, pointing into open sky. Beyond it
twenty feet or so of concrete wharf before
the blue-black water of the lake. Danny said
that he could make it, easy. We said
never. He said case of beer, put up
or shut up. We said
asshole. Frank said first he should go get our beer
because he wasn't going to get it paralysed or dead.
Everybody got up, taking this excuse
to stretch and smoke and pace the roof
from eaves to peak, discussing gravity
and Steve McQueen, who never used a stunt man, Danny's
life expectancy, and whether that should be a case
of Export or O'Keefe's. We knew what this was –
ongoing argument to fray
the tedium of work akin to filter vs. plain,

stick shift vs. automatic, condom vs.
pulling out in time. We flicked our butts toward the lake
and got back to the job. And then, amid the squat,
hammer, heft, no one saw him go. Suddenly he
wasn't there, just his boots
with his hammer stuck inside one like a heavy-headed
flower. Back then it was bizarre that,
after all that banter, he should be so silent,
so inward with it just to
run off into sky. Later I thought,
cool. Still later I think it makes sense his voice should
sink back into breath and breath
devote itself to taking in whatever air
might have to say on that short flight between the roof
and the rest of his natural life.

Lift

To stand with mind akimbo where the wind
riffles the ridge. Slow,
slow jazz: it must begin
before the instrument with bones
dreaming themselves hollow and the dusk
rising in them like a sloth
ascending. Moon,
night after night rehearsing shades of pause
and spill, sifting into reed beds,
silvering the fine hairs on your arms, making
rhythm out of light and nothing, making
months. What have I ever made of life or it
of me? All I ever asked for
was to be remembered constantly
by everything I ever touched.
                                    Now I need
a scrap of night to wrap up in and sleep who
knows how many eons until something –
maybe dotted, maybe ragged,
maybe dun – unfolds. Something quick.
Something helpful to the air.

Drag

But, however,
on the other hand.
Not gravity, that irresistible embrace,
but its photograph, packed in your bag
with too many shirts. Drag
wants to dress the nakedness of speed, to hold clothes
in the slipstream until body reincarnates, then
it will be sorry, won't it?
Yes it will. It will be as sorry as the
square of its upward urge.
                      When I approached the edge
it seemed one gentle waft
would carry me across, the brief lilt
of a Horned Lark up from roadside gravel
into the adjacent field.
                 However,
on the other hand. It occurred to me that,
unlike Horned Larks, who are imagination,
I was mostly memory, which,
though photogenic and nutritious, rich
with old-time goodness, is notoriously
heavier than air.

Forest Moon

(June: Williamstown, Ontario)

The light, though full of motion,
neither falls nor pours
into the clearing, but as it enters, ebbs
back into itself:
                  we float off from the porch,
letting its tug entice us
to the path. What used to be basswood leaves
are silver gloves that beckon,
this way, this way,
down to the abandoned tracks.
The old rails,
who spend their days becoming rust,
are glimmering with distance, tracks left
by some ardent creature we have just missed seeing.
Fortunately.
               Where can they be pointing?
Not to Cornwall, Ontario.
Not to any place I'd care to put a name to.

Song for the Song of the White-Throated Sparrow

Before it can stop itself, the mind
has leapt up inferences, crag to crag,
the obvious arpeggio. Where there is a doorbell
there must be a door – a door
meant to be opened from inside.
Door means house means – wait a second –
but already it is standing on a threshold previously
known to be thin air, gawking. The Black Spruce
point to it: clarity,
melting into ordinary morning, true
north. Where the sky is just a name,
a way to pitch a little tent in space and sleep
for five unnumbered seconds.

Glide

Sometimes the eye brims
over with desire and pours
into its flight path:

this is gaze, and glide
is when the body follows,
flowing into river, when the heart,

turning the word "forever"
into plainsong,
learns to purr, knowing

the most important
lesson of grade four
is the blank but pointed

page, the pure wish that we
sharpen into dart and send
skimming the desks and out

the window, through the schoolyard
with its iron jungle gym, across
the traffic we must always

stop and look both
ways for, meanwhile, gazing
at us from its prehistoric perch, a small

but enterprising lizard
is about to launch itself
into the warm arms of the Mesozoic afternoon.

Luna Moth Meditation

How foolish to think death's pale flag
would be rectangular and stark, rather than this
scrap of wedding dress symmetrically ripped
and sent back, cruelly,
to be his deaf and nearly mouthless
messenger. As it unfolds – gorgeous, appalling –
I can feel my mind fill up
with its own weight, as though
suffering unexpected snowfall.
Think of a Eurydice who makes it
all the way, following an Orpheus
with more self-discipline,
and probably less talent, just to find herself
forbidden that huge
other eros:
                how she craves the darkness and her legs
drink down into dirt. And that moment
in the sickroom when the dead one's been removed
and the Kleenex in the waste can
starts to metamorphose, tissue
taking wing, wing
taking the very drape and slope of grief
and struggling out the door.

Feather

The mystery of feather
is the birth of listening in the late Jurassic,
how out of ordinary hearing came this quick
attention to the air, how between those fine
aspiring lizards and the wind there was this give
and give, that thickening of nothings
into lift, and the mystery

of feather is the womb of song, inside
the strict routine of scales it stirs and
shrugs its small shoulders,
stretches its trapezoids, fingers its new
curves and the

mystery of feather is to think of an infinity of hairs like
prehistoric Velcro zipping up to catch and hold and
spill the wind and the mystery of

feather is the birth of the caress, that moment
when my skin begins to bloom toward your fingers, who are
skimming, like Sanderlings across the sand,
the incredulous articulations of my back.

The Book of Moonlight

"*The book of moonlight is not written yet.*"
    –Wallace Stevens

Arriviste, you are the reader
who has come too early, or too late,
and lingers in the spill of light
which might be aftermath, might be
anticipation. Plots that once were
furtive among leaves have long since
hatched from narrative into a sort of
disembodied drinking, a long-distance runner smoothly
shedding feet as she grows more and more
mercurial. How about you? Will you also shed the wish
not to be mistaken as your breath flits
in and out among the rumours and the cat
follows its whiskers into pure nuance?
In the scene you've missed, or are
about to witness, desire
and departure rendezvous. No hero happens,
unless it is you, the creature at the cusp of change,
the avid unabashed *voyeur*.

About the Poets and Translators

Yehuda Amichai (1924–2000) was a writer with an international reputation. He was born in Germany and emigrated with his parents to Palestine in 1936. Best known for his poetry, he was the recipient of numerous awards, including the Israel Prize, his country's highest honour. *Open Closed Open* was published in Israel in the original Hebrew in 1998, and the English translation from which the selections for this anthology are drawn was published in 2000 by Harcourt, Inc.

Chana Bloch, author of the prize-winning *Mrs. Dumpty* and co-translator of the *Selected Poetry of Yehuda Amichai* and the *Song of Songs*, directs the Creative Writing Program at Mills College, Oakland, CA. Her co-translation of Yehuda Amichai's *Open Closed Open* was published in 2000 by Harcourt, Inc.

Robert Bringhurst is one of Canada's most respected poets and one of its most probing cultural historians. He is a skilled linguist who has worked for many years with Native American texts and is the author of *Story as Sharp as a Knife*, Volume 1 of the trilogy *Masterworks of the Classical Haida*. He translated *Nine Visits to the Mythworld* from Haida, originally phonetically transcribed by a young American anthropologist on the Northwest Coast of North America in 1900. *Nine Visits to the Mythworld* was published in 2000 by Douglas & McIntyre in Canada and the University of Nebraska Press in the U.S.

Anne Carson lives in Montreal, where she is Director of Graduate Studies, Classics, at McGill University. Her first book published in Britain, *Glass and God*, was shortlisted for the 1998 Forward Prize; her second, *Autobiography of Red*, was shortlisted for the National Book Critics Circle Award and the T. S. Eliot Prize. She has won the Lannan Award, the Pushcart Prize, and, most recently, the MacArthur Fellowship. *Men in the Off Hours* was published in 2000 by Vintage Canada, Jonathan Cape in the U.K., Alfred A. Knopf in the U.S., and Cape/Random House in Australia.

Paul Celan (1920–1970) is widely regarded as Europe's greatest postwar poet. Born in Romania, Celan survived the Holocaust and settled in Paris after the war, where he remained until his death. Celan spoke at least six languages and worked as a translator of French, Russian, and English literature. He wrote his poetry solely in German. Among his major poems is *Death Fugue* that evokes the horrors of the Holocaust. *Glottal Stop: 101 Poems by Paul Celan* was published in 2000 by Wesleyan University Press.

Fanny Howe is Professor of Writing and Literature at the University of California, San Diego. One of the best and most respected experimental poets in the United States, she is the author of more than twenty books of fiction and poetry. Boston is the setting for some of her early poems, and Ireland, the birthplace of Howe's mother, is the home of *O'Clock*, a spiritually piquant series of short poems included in *Selected Poems*. *Fanny Howe: Selected Poems* was published in 2000 by University of California Press.

Chana Kronfeld, who teaches Hebrew and Comparative Literature at the University of California, Berkeley, writes about Yehuda Amichai in her *On the Margins of Modernism*, winner of the Modern Languages Association's Scaglione Prize. Her co-translation of Yehuda Amichai's *Open Closed Open* was published in 2000 by Harcourt, Inc.

Heather McHugh is Milliman Distinguished Writer-in-Residence at the University of Washington. In addition to six acclaimed books of poetry, including most recently, *The Father of the Predicaments*, and the collection of essays *Broken English: Poetry and Partiality*, she has translated Euripides' *Cyclops* and poems by Jean Follain. Her co-translation of *Glottal Stop: 101 Poems by Paul Celan* was published in 2000 by Wesleyan University Press.

Don McKay won Canada's Governor General's Award for poetry for *Night Field* and *Another Gravity*. Two other collections were shortlisted for the Governor General's Award: *Apparatus* and *Birding, or desire*, which won him the Canadian Authors Association Award for Poetry. He lives in Victoria, British Columbia. *Another Gravity* was published in 2000 by McClelland & Stewart.

Les Murray was born in Australia in 1938. He is the author of twenty-three titles published in Australia and several in the United States and

England. He won the U.K.'s T. S. Eliot Prize for *Subhuman Redneck Poems* and *Fredy Neptune: A Novel in Verse.* He has been honoured by the Australian government with the Medal of the Order of Australia for his services to literature and the Queen's Gold Medal for Poetry. He has won numerous Australian National Book Council Awards and the Australian National Poetry Award, among other prizes. *Learning Human: Selected Poems* was published in 2000 by Farrar, Straus & Giroux in the U.S. and Carcanet Press Limited in the U.K.

Nikolai Popov teaches English and Comparative Literature at the University of Washington in Seattle. A James Joyce scholar and translator, he co-translated with Heather McHugh a collection of the poems of Blaga Dimitrova. His co-translation of *Glottal Stop: 101 Poems by Paul Celan* was published in 2000 by Wesleyan University Press.

Acknowledgements

The publishers thank the following for their kind permission to reprint the work contained in this volume:

"The Amen Stone," "I Foretell the Days of Yore," and "Houses (Plural); Love (Singular)" from *Open Closed Open* by Yehuda Amichai (translated by Chana Bloch and Chana Kronfeld) are reprinted by permission of Harcourt Inc.

The selections from *Glottal Stop: 101 Poems by Paul Celan* (translated by Nikolai Popov & Heather McHugh) are reprinted by permission of Wesleyan University Press.

The selections from *Fanny Howe: Selected Poems* are reprinted by permission of the author and University of California Press.

"An Absolutely Ordinary Rainbow," "The Quality of Sprawl," "Nocturne," "The Tin Wash Dish," "The Cows on Killing Day," and "The International Terminal" from *Learning Human: Selected Poems* by Les Murray. Copyright © 2000 Les Murray. Reprinted by permission of Farrar, Straus and Giroux, LLC, and Carcanet Press Ltd.

"Epitaph: Zion," "New Rule," "Father's Old Blue Cardigan," "TV Men: Sappho," "TV Men: Lazarus," and "Epitaph: Thaw" from *Men in the Off Hours* by Anne Carson, copyright © 2000 by Anne Carson. Used by permission of Alfred A. Knopf, a division of Random House, Inc., and Jonathan Cape.

"The Way the Weather Chose to Be Born" from *Nine Visits to the Mythworld* by Ghandl of the Qayahl Llaanas (translated by Robert Bringhurst) is reprinted by permission of Douglas & McIntyre and University of Nebraska Press.

"Sometimes a Voice (1)," "Lift," "Drag," "Forest Moon," "Song for the Song of the White-Throated Sparrow," "Glide," "Luna Moth Meditation," "Feather," and "The Book of Moonlight" from *Another Gravity* by Don McKay are reprinted by permission of McClelland & Stewart, Ltd.